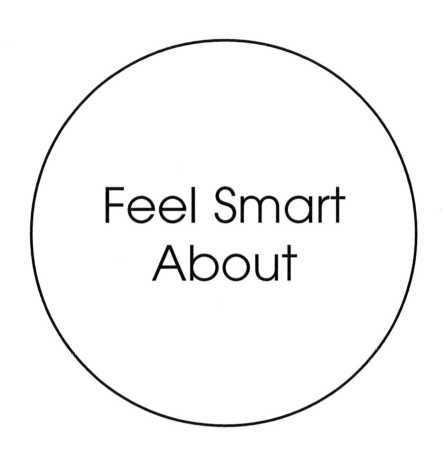

Feel Smart About

Feel Smart About

Managing and Investing Your Money in Your 20s

Christian Echavarria

iUniverse, Inc.
New York Lincoln Shanghai

**Feel Smart About
Managing and Investing Your Money in Your 20s**

iUniverse books may be ordered through booksellers or by contacting:

iUniverse
2021 Pine Lake Road, Suite 100
Lincoln, NE 68512
www.iuniverse.com
1-800-Authors (1-800-288-4677)

The information, ideas, and suggestions in this book are not intended to render professional advice. Before following any suggestions contained in this book, you should consult your personal accountant or other financial advisor. Neither the author nor the publisher shall be liable or responsible for any loss or damage allegedly arising as a consequence of your use or application of any information or suggestions in this book.

Cover Design and Illustration by Tom Mosser (www.mosserart.com)
Book Illustrations by Tom Mosser
Chart content and design by Christian Echavarria

ISBN: 978-0-595-41401-7 (pbk)
ISBN: 978-0-595-67904-1 (cloth)
ISBN: 978-0-595-85752-4 (ebk)

Printed in the United States of America

To my wife, Laurel, with all my love and gratitude.

Contents

Acknowledgments

Crafting a story that can draw a reader in to join characters as they gain everyday, practical knowledge, experience, and insights is an incredible challenge. Such a project requires the help of many talented and committed individuals.

I would like to acknowledge the talent of Erik David Price and Tom Mosser in helping to create and illustrate a meaningful real-life story and experience; the relentless commitment of my avid investor and father-in-law, Dr. James Ransom; and my partner Mark Gensheimer and his wife, Annie, and my trusted friend Rich Redeker, for their help in simplifying complex matters in ways that make the reader take action.

Finally, the many employees and friends at Invesmart, who worked so hard to always find a better way to help our valuable clients manage and invest their money to build a prosperous and secure future, simply cannot go without recognition—especially Kent Baur, Mark Hutter, Brian Christ, Rob Rossi, Leah Beck, Erin Eddins, Cheryl Talerico, Bob Lee, Mark Sommers, Renee Courey, Debra Irby-Gibson, Rick Rocco, Brad Ferguson, Joe Gummo, Jeff Corbitt, Sherry Palinkas, and Tim Miller.

One

Uncertainty and Indecision

We carve our path in life by the choices we make—wealth is a choice we make.

Jack Myers gasped for air as his fingertips began to slip from the slimy brick ledge, the only thing holding his head above the well water. His eyes scanned from left to right looking for a way out and then veered below him. Deep in the water, he could see mountains of coins staring up at him, unfulfilled wishes beckoning him to join them beneath the water's surface. As his hands went numb and his biceps shook with exhaustion, he saw his young life playing out before his eyes. *Is this going to be the end?* Jack thought to himself. Not if he could help it. He gave a series of kicks with his legs in an attempt to propel himself up and onto the ledge, but he was dressed in his cook's uniform and the weight of the water soaking into it overtook him; his hands lost their grip and he fell beneath the water.

As he floated downward, suddenly, he heard a voice in the darkness. "Jack, no matter how many times you've fallen, no matter how desperate the situation, there is always a way out. There is always a solution."

Jack looked up to the light at the top of the water and swam toward it with every last ounce of energy his muscles could muster. In the same moment that his face broke the surface of the water, he awoke from the nightmare with beads of sweat rolling down his forehead and the tip of his nose. In the silence of the night, Jack heard his father's advice ringing in his ears: *There is always a solution. Just take a step back and think through it.*

As he sat on the edge of his bed, Jack's mind moved on to bigger and better things. He felt a sudden rush of excitement, knowing that tomorrow would be his first day in the real world. Having just graduated from culinary school, he was ready for his new job as sous-chef at the posh new Mondrian Restaurant and what he hoped would be the first step in realizing his lifelong dream of building a chain of gourmet restaurants.

Jack leaned forward and stretched, readying himself to face the day. As he pulled himself into a standing position, the anxiety from his terrible dream reappeared and Jack felt a sudden sense of uncertainty about money.

*   *   *

Jack Myers is just like any one of us in the early years of our careers, regardless of personal situation, career, or income level. During these early years, we devote our focus and attention to living a little and finding our *life compass*, our personal and professional directions in life. Frankly, we've sacrificed so much to reach this point—after all those years of enduring the student life—that we feel the need to live a little once we finally enter the workplace.

Now, we all have the best of intentions. We plan to save our newly found income, but it seems we keep finding things that need to be taken care of first: that old clunker needs to be replaced with a newer car; we're tired of eating on top of cardboard boxes in our apartment, so we furnish it; eating in and having to cook is so much more of a hassle than picking something up on the road or enjoying a meal out with friends.

These are times of mixed emotions. We are excited about our personal and professional prospects, but soon enough we find that we're stretching our paychecks to afford our everyday needs and to pay off debts.

Many times, we mistakenly hope that time will take care of all these financial problems we are creating if only we can just hang on … and then, like Jack, we suddenly find ourselves kicking hard just to keep our heads above water.

These are the *best* times, however, to carve our own path in life and choose to build wealth.

*   *   *

Just as Jack was about to step into the shower, his cell phone rang. On the other end of the line was his old friend George Johnson. Jack and George met at Peter's Pub during their freshman year in college in Pittsburgh. George studied computer science at Carnegie Mellon University while Jack was a liberal-arts student at the University of Pittsburgh before he dropped out his junior year to enroll in culinary school. It was their love of Steelers football that brought them together.

George had finished up his degree at Carnegie Mellon three years ago and chose to stay in Pittsburgh, close to the university, to build his first company, an on-demand podcast-based training service for corporations.

"Hello?"

"Jack, it's George. How are you feeling this morning?"

"I'm feeling good," replied Jack, walking toward the shower.

"I wanted to see if you want to grab a cup of coffee. Maybe we could go over what we were talking about last night? I hope what I told you makes sense and helps you stop worrying about money," said George.

"I wouldn't exactly say it helped me stop worrying, George," replied Jack, a bit frustrated. "I get half of it. I get the part about managing my career. I am definitely passionate about what I do. I'm following my dream—"

"That's funny," said George, interrupting Jack. "I thought that managing money would be the easiest part for you. I mean, it's just a recipe, right?"

"We'll see about that. I'll see you down at the coffee shop in fifteen minutes."

Jack stepped into the shower and leaned forward, letting the water run over his face. He thought about his conversation with George, his first day of work only a day away, and last night's dream. Most important, he wondered how he was ever going to find his own recipe to get on track saving and investing.

*   *   *

Building wealth is about managing our careers and the money we make. It all starts with the understanding that we build wealth primarily for two reasons: 1) to build prosperity and 2) to afford a comfortable retirement. Saving and investing to build prosperity is what we do to improve the quality and independence in our lives. Each of us measures quality and independence in our own terms—to some it means being able to afford big-ticket expenses, such as a dream home or supporting a favorite charity. To others it might mean making money *work for us* so that we don't have to *work for it*.

We save and invest for retirement because, at some point in the future, we will choose to stop working and will need to replace the salary we currently earn. Saving and investing to afford a comfortable retirement is an obligation we have to ourselves. It is important to realize that we have no choice but to get on track saving and investing for retirement. We will be depending on it for survival in the later years of our life—considering how much longer people live with every passing decade, saving and investing is becoming increasingly more important.

The secret to building wealth is really an easy formula. Just as George explained to Jack, it's a recipe.

*   *   *

Jack stepped out into the sunshine, his favorite gold Steelers cap covering his still-damp hair, and walked quickly down to the coffee shop on the corner. George was already sitting at one of the sidewalk tables, leaning forward to take a sip of iced tea as Jack walked up.

"Hey, buddy, I'm ready for that amazing recipe you have for me," said Jack with a smile on his face.

"I'm sure the best new sous-chef in town can handle it," said George with a laugh.

"Seriously," said Jack, "I'm worried about how I'm supposed to stretch my paycheck to cover all of my living expenses *and* pay off debts. How am I supposed to have enough money left over so that I can start saving?"

"Let me give you a different way to think about money," explains George. "You know that because I'm running my own business, I'm not making much money.

But the way I see it, I'm earning all the money I need to build a fortune as long as I don't spend any of it."

"Now you're just being cute," said Jack.

"No, really. You're thinking about money the wrong way. Instead of thinking about how much you'll have left over to save, you need to think in terms of how much you'll have left over to spend."

*   *   *

Most of us think about or budget our money in terms of our spending needs. We start by asking how much we want to spend on different items—clothing, vacations, car payments—and then we look at what is left over to build wealth. When we have a spending mindset, we spend more as we earn more. We are more likely to find a buried treasure than to *spend* ourselves into wealth.

Those who will be successful building wealth, like George, start by asking how much they want to save and invest and then manage their spending accordingly. When you have a *wealth mindset*, you save and invest more as you earn more.

Most of us start our careers with a spending mindset and become accustomed to a lifestyle we enjoy. Maybe we spend to keep up with our peers. It's not easy to shift from a spending mindset to a wealth mindset. However, it is *easiest* during the *early years* of our careers, since most of our spending commitments are short-lived and more flexible.

*   *   *

"Oh, I get it," said Jack, leaning back in his chair. "You want me to first decide how much I will save and invest, and then see what's left over to feed myself. It sounds like a plan for starvation."

"Jack, what matters is that you have the right mindset, even if it means you only choose to start by saving and investing one dollar. The most important thing is that you stop that spending mindset of yours."

"Listen, I've got to run. I'll see you later today, around five," said Jack, trying to dismiss the conversation.

"Well, before you go, let me tell you one more thing," said George. "As a first step, why don't you just try to think about what you need to get on track saving and investing?"

"I will, I will," said Jack, putting on his sunglasses.

"Jack, I know you too well. Once you know what to do, you're like a pit bull. You won't let go of it."

*   *   *

Each stage of our lives requires a unique recipe for financial success—a recipe we can understand, believe in, and commit to. As we succeed at each stage, the subsequent stages become easier and more within our reach.

When we start our careers, it's easy to get distracted from our financial responsibilities. We're trying to organize our lives—buying new clothes, upgrading furniture, buying a few luxuries we work so hard to reach. The main challenge during the early years is to get on track saving and investing.

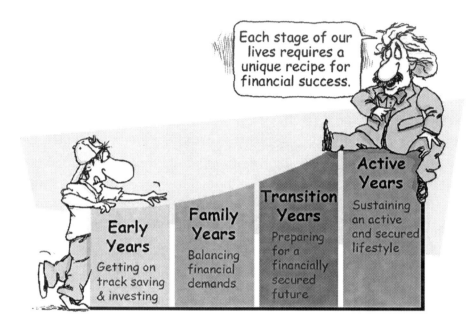

At this stage, what's important is that Jack comes up with a plan. He will have plenty of time to tackle the different challenges that he faces as his life evolves. For example, when he finds out that he's making progress saving and investing and enters into his family years, a new set of financial demands will come into the picture. Maybe he'll become a homeowner, or perhaps he'll have children and begin thinking about their college educations. At that point, he'll have to focus on balancing his financial demands. He'll want to satisfy his present needs while continuing to build financial wealth. When his children graduate from college, Jack will begin thinking about retirement, his active years. And he'll have to become even more serious about his future. During these transitional years, he'll take inventory of his financial readiness and, during those years before retirement, focus on closing any financial gaps he may still have. This will ensure Jack's financial future is secure. Once Jack moves into his active years, he'll want to live out his hopes and dreams. He'll focus on managing his income from his nest egg to sustain an active and secure lifestyle.

While it's helpful to see a roadmap of the future, it's important right now for Jack to gain the understanding that each stage demands a focus on the right recipe for financial success. Success at each stage makes the stages that follow that much easier. Conversely, failure at any stage builds up new challenges that must then be faced. For Jack, all that matters at this point is to get on track.

Two

Always a Solution

We accomplish what we know. Let's know what we need to accomplish.

Busy in the kitchen, Jack was looking through his notebooks, trying to track down his recipe for stuffed tenderloin to get ready for that evening's get-together when his phone rang again. This time, it was Linda Cruz.

Jack met Linda through George in their junior year, just as Jack was transferring to culinary school. Linda and George were an inseparable pair during their last two years at school but parted ways before graduation. The joke among their friends was that Linda and George had fallen in love because opposites attract, but parted ways because their differences drove them insane.

Unlike George, who believed that people should follow their passions and dreams and patiently stay on target, Linda was impatient and always ready to get a jump on the next opportunity with no clear direction in mind.

After school, Linda quickly became a star consultant with a large national firm and was fast-tracked to engagement manager, a role typically reserved for consultants with MBA degrees. She was highly driven and very comfortable in the no-nonsense, competitive corporate world.

Linda had recently come back to Pittsburgh for a three-month consulting engagement to help a local company improve its service center.

"Jack, it's Linda. When do you want me to show up at your place?" asked Linda without even waiting for Jack to say hello.

"Hey, slow down," answered Jack. "You know, George is also coming tonight," said Jack, knowing that Linda liked to get to the bottom of things quickly.

"I figured he would be."

"Is that going to be okay?" asked Jack.

"Well, we haven't talked since I left Pittsburgh," said Linda, sounding a little more tense than usual.

"I just talked to him and asked him to come by around five. Does that time work for you?" asked Jack, trying to move the conversation along.

"I have a review with a client this afternoon at two, but I'm planning on keeping it short and to the point. Five o'clock should be fine for me."

"Linda, before you go, let me ask you a question, since you're a numbers person."

"What's on your mind?" asked Linda.

"How do I figure out what I need to do to get on track saving and investing?"

"What are you talking about?" asked Linda, wondering why Jack was worrying about this right now.

"Well, I've been worried about money with my new job, and George suggested that I need to figure out how to get on track," explained Jack, a little embarrassed about asking.

"That sounds like George," said Linda. "I guess he told you the best way to manage your career is to follow your passions and dreams."

"Well, actually, he did."

"Listen to me, Jack. You can't have such a naïve view of the world. You need to learn to become opportunistic with your career."

"Can we not go there right now? I'm really just interested in—"

"Jack, wait," interrupted Linda. "These two things go together."

"I know, I know."

"Okay. I don't want you to get all tangled up in numbers," said Linda, speaking in a tone that Jack imagined she must use a lot at work. "I want you to develop a common sense understanding of what you need to do. You've got to start by defining your priorities."

*   *   *

When we begin to examine our priorities in order to get on track saving and investing, we need to think in terms of *cascading priorities*. We want to start saving for our most difficult and longest-term priority first—retirement. Once we are on track saving for retirement, before we can focus on saving to build prosperity in our lives, we need to reduce expensive debts.

Just like water filling each bowl and cascading down, overflowing into the next, we have to address each priority before moving on. Only once the first bowl is filled can the next begin to take on water. The same goes for how we distribute our income.

It's important to start saving first for our most difficult and longest-term objective because it can be nearly impossible to get on track if we start too late or save too little. Additionally, we need to eliminate any expensive debt, such as credit card balances that make us work for somebody else's prosperity, before we can pursue our own.

*   *   *

"Before we get all caught up in details, you need to get a good sense of what to accomplish," continued Linda. "Let me ask you a question. How big of a nest egg do you think you're going to need to retire comfortably?"

"Whoa," interrupted Jack. "Isn't it a little early to worry about retirement?"

"Actually, as counterintuitive as it may seem, you need to get your toughest and most long-term goals on track," explained Linda. "I'm not saying that you need to accumulate your entire nest egg before you do anything else. I'm just telling you that you're going to need to get the ball rolling."

"Okay, but I don't have the foggiest idea how to figure out what kind of nest egg I'm going to need."

"There are actually some really simple formulas that I can show you that will figure all of that out for you. What I can tell you is that it's going to be a lot, which is why you should get going on that right away."

*   *   *

Getting on track preparing for retirement is our most important priority during our early years. Since it is difficult to even plan beyond next year, thinking about retirement is unnatural. A short conversation with a trusted relative or friend who is close to retirement or retired should put to rest any notion that retirement is far away. We need to ask them how long it took them to reach their current age and ask them what they would have done differently with their finances. They will likely give us two answers: 1) I reached my current age in a blink of an eye, and 2) start saving for retirement with your very first paycheck.

While retirement may seem a long way off, it's important to get our toughest and longest-term financial objectives on track before addressing our easier and more short-term ones.

So how big a nest egg do we really need for retirement? To answer this question precisely, we need to know how successful we're going to be during our career and the lifestyle to which we'll become accustomed. With this information, we can figure out how much it will cost us to maintain that lifestyle once we reach retirement—an impossible question to answer with precision so early in our careers. There is, however, a simple formula to get a reasonable estimate of the size of the nest egg we'll need at retirement.

We can get started any time with a reasonable estimate. What is most important is that we review our estimate periodically as we make progress with our career
and adjust our level of savings as needed to stay on track.

The formula is based on a simple notion. When we
retire, we want to draw about 4 percent of our nest egg
annually to cover our living expenses that are not covered
by Social Security.[1]

---

1   Some people may have other sources of income during retire-
     ment, such as a pension plan from their employer. However, in
     today's environment, pension plans are typically an exception
     with younger employees and becoming more so.

The 4 percent is based on the idea that we want to balance drawing enough money to satisfy our financial needs, but not draw too much that we run the risk of out-living our nest egg.[2]

The formula also assumes that our expenses at retirement will be 85 percent of our preretirement salary and that the strained Social Security system will only cover about one-third of our retirement expenses.[3]

As we continue the discussion, keep in mind that, at this stage, a big debate about assumptions is not critical. It is important that we get a keener sense of the effort needed to save for retirement. Saving for retirement is a lifelong effort that requires an early start and the discipline to remain committed. As we become more successful in our career and our lifestyle begins to change, we can make adjustments to these assumptions.

---

2   Some financial planners may suggest only drawing 4 percent while other more aggressive planners may suggest drawing 5 percent. At this stage in your career, it is appropriate to use a 4-percent-draw assumption and a retirement age of sixty-five to develop a reasonable estimate of the size of your nest egg.

3   The range of assumptions used in the financial planning industry for the level of expenses at retirement as a percentage of preretirement salary typically ranges from 70 to 100 percent. Social Security coverage estimates may range typically from 20 to 50 percent based on salary levels. The higher percentage is typically associated with lower income retirees.

Regardless of what we assume, we are going to find out primarily one thing: *we need a big nest egg.*

Let's see how the formula works: we know our current salary (or salary we expect if we are just entering the workforce). All that remains is an estimate of our career success—or how much bigger we expect our salary to get by the time we reach retirement.

If we expect to experience typical career success, at the age of sixty-five, we can expect our salary to be approximately three to three and a half times our salary in our twenties.[4] Therefore, if our current salary is, for example, $30,000, we can develop a reasonable estimate of our nest egg by multiplying that $30,000 by three to three and a half and then again by fifteen,[5] which equals approximately $1.5 million.

The calculation shows that, as a rule of thumb, our nest egg at retirement needs to be approximately fifty times our current salary during our twenties. Therefore,

---

4   Assumes a long-term average annual salary growth of 3 percent.

5   The factor of fifteen is derived from the assumptions as follows: One multiplied by the 85-percent ratio of expenses at retirement as a percentage of pre-retirement salary, multiplied by the 70-percent income at retirement not covered from Social Security, and divided by the 4-percent-draw assumption.

we can just multiply our current salary by fifty to develop a reasonable estimate of the required nest egg.

Nest Egg

Fifty times your salary in your 20s to retire at 65!

Salary in your 20s

There's no magic in the calculation of our required nest egg. Again, what is important is that we start with reasonable assumptions, update those assumptions as we learn more about our career success, and always have a reasonable and clear picture in our mind of the size of the nest egg that we are going to need.

*　　　　　*　　　　　*

"Okay, so what do I need to do to get on track?" asked Jack again.

"I've gone over these numbers many times and talked to many financial advisors. The bottom line is that you need to start saving and start saving now. It has to start with your first paycheck," continued Linda.

*   *   *

As financial projections show (and most financial planners agree), when we are in our early twenties, we need to save at least 6 percent or, ideally, 10 percent of our salary for retirement to get on track. Then we should increase our savings by 1 percent every time we get a chance, such as every time we get a salary increase.

By the time we reach thirty-five years of age, we should be saving as close to 15 percent of our salary as we possibly can for retirement.

If we expect the typical career success, these levels of savings will put us on a path to accumulate the nest egg we'll need when we retire to afford the lifestyle we'll be accustomed to.

It is important, however, to review periodically how we are doing. To assess whether we are staying on track, we should have in our retirement savings account an amount equivalent to about one time our salary by the time we are thirty and an amount equivalent to about two times our salary by the time we are thirty-five.[6]

6 Assumes investment returns of 8.6 percent for the first twenty-eight years declining to 7.2 percent, as the individual gets closer to retirement and moves to more conservative investments. Returns calculated using the following assumptions: long-term average annual real stocks returns of 6.8, long-term average annual real bonds returns of 3.5 percent, long-term average annual real cash investments returns of 2.9 percent, and long-term average annual inflation of 2.5 percent.

For example, if our salary has grown to $35,000 by the time we are thirty, we should have accumulated about $35,000 in our retirement accounts.

There are several reasons we may get behind, for example, we start saving late, we save too little, or the financial markets perform poorly. We may also get behind if our career success is better than we expected (i.e., we get behind because we are going to need an even bigger nest egg in the future to support an even better lifestyle at retirement than we initially expected).

If we find ourselves behind in our mid-thirties, let's not push the panic button. Let's make sure that we are setting our savings level as close to 15 percent of our salary as we possibly can for retirement. If we are behind because we started saving late, we saved too little, or the financial markets have performed poorly, we also need to continue to increase our savings level by 2 percent at every available opportunity.

If we find ourselves behind because our career success is much better than we expected and we foresee this success to continue into the future, then we need to accelerate even more. We can then increase our savings level by 3 percent (instead of 2 percent) every opportunity we have. In this situation, since we are doing so well financially, it should be easier to increase our savings.

*   *   *

"Okay, I'm beginning to get the picture," said Jack, sounding satisfied.

"There are some other things you should keep in mind," added Linda. "Do you have any expensive credit card debt or other debt outside of your school loans?"

"Nope, just the school loan," said Jack.

"Well, in that case, your next priority needs to be building prosperity in your life, which, in your case, means that chain of restaurants that you've been dreaming about."

*   *   *

A quick review: we build financial wealth to afford a comfortable retirement and build prosperity in our lives. It is important to separate the two, both mentally and physically, because they each require different saving and investing approaches.

Survival in the later years of our lives is dependent on saving and investing for retirement now. There is no room for saving-failure or investment speculation. On the other hand, saving and investing to build prosperity in our lives provides more room for flexibility and creativity when it comes to how we accumulate and invest our money.

To build prosperity, we first need to make sure we stop working to build someone else's prosperity. That means we need to reduce and eliminate expensive debt. Except for an emergency and business-related investments, there are only two situations that justify going into personal debt: 1) smart investing in the purchase of a home; 2) investing in our own education.

We all know that there are taxes and likely appreciation benefits from owning a home; however, a poor investment on the wrong home or overspending on a home we cannot afford may overshadow these benefits entirely. If we plan to invest in a home, let's do our homework. Let's approach the process of investing in a home as if we were making our largest and most important invest-ment—because that's exactly what we're doing.

The details of "how to invest in the right home, in the right location, and at the right price" are beyond this book, but we need to take the time to study how to make this very important investment and get good advice from a trusted real estate agent.

If we are carrying school-loan debt, let's be realistic. We carry that debt because we've made one of our smartest investments—our education. For example, in the United States, the typical (median) income of individuals holding a college education is more than twice the typical income of individuals holding just a high school education.[7]

It is never too late to pursue specialized training (e.g., culinary school) or a college education to build prosper-ity, given the increasing availability of specialized train-ing and college programs for working individuals and the flexibility of education online.

---

7   Source: Federal Reserve Board, 2004 Survey of Consumer Finances.

Beyond a good investment in a home and education, any other debt should be viewed as working for someone else's prosperity—avoid it, or if you have it, reduce and eliminate it.

It's very difficult to build prosperity in our lives without a shift from a spending mindset to a wealth mindset. There's no single formula to determine how much we should save for prosperity in addition to what we are saving for retirement. At a minimum, and based on what most individuals in their twenties can afford, we should start saving 5 percent of our salaries to build prosperity.

As we look at what Jack should start saving to build financial wealth in his twenties, he should start by saving, ideally, a total of 15 percent of his salary—ideally, 10 percent of that in his nest egg account for retirement and 5 percent in an separate account to build prosperity.

Start by saving and investing, ideally, 15% of your salary to build financial wealth.

Saving 15 percent of our salary at this stage of our lives is not a trivial amount, but a meaningful effort toward changing how we thinks about money—*a meaningful effort toward getting on track saving and investing.*

*   *   *

"I can't tell you how much money you're going to need to set aside to build your chain of restaurants," said Linda. "It really doesn't even matter at this stage. What matters is that you get started so you can change how you think about money."

"Let me stop you right there," said Jack. "I already got the lecture from George on having a wealth mindset."

"Do you believe it?" asked Linda.

"Yes, I do," answered Jack.

"Good! As long as you start setting money aside with your very first paycheck for retirement and your chain of restaurants, then you'll be on your way."

Jack hung up the phone and got ready to go to the farmer's market to pick up some ingredients for tonight's dinner. As he walked out the door, a slight smile appeared on his face. He sensed that his financial recipe was beginning to take shape. Now he needed to find out how to invest what he saved.

Three

Commitment

Commitment and discipline are the ingredients of great investors. Let's develop and commit to an investor style.

Waiting for his friends to arrive, Jack scanned the ingredients organized on the kitchen counter. He smirked as he quietly plotted to recruit his friends to help him prepare the evening feast in order to keep George and Linda occupied.

A few minutes before five, the doorbell rang. Jack opened the door to greet Kim Hu and Jim Anderson. Both Kim and Jim had known Jack since their days at the University of Pittsburgh and the three had remained close friends. Jim was a well-known national artist who painted professional athletes in action. Knowing that making it as an artist—his dream and passion—would be challenging, Jim developed a cunning ability to find pockets of opportunity in the art world that managed to pay well. Kim was an investment research analyst for a national investment advisory firm. She was quick to explain that her job was to help her clients to invest, not hunt for treasures or read crystal balls.

"We're a bit early," said Kim, giving Jack a hug and a quick kiss.

"Well, come in, this should be a fun night ... I think."

"I understand you're bringing them together after three years," said Kim, sharing Jack's concern about having George and Linda in the same room again.

"So what do we have here?" asked Jim, trying to lighten up the mood as he walked into the kitchen and saw the food spread out on the counter.

"We're going to be making stuffed tenderloin," said Jack with pride.

"This looks like a five-star restaurant spread," said Kim. "I would expect nothing less from you."

"I'll bet you're excited about tomorrow," said Jim. "You've been working hard for this one."

"On one hand, I'm ready to start my dream," said Jack. "On the other, I have the usual feelings about moving into the real world."

"Let me guess," said Kim. "You're worried about money."

"How do you know?" asked Jack.

"Oh, come on. I've been there too," said Kim. "What's on your mind?"

"Let's not ruin our night talking about money," answered Jack.

"Actually, let's talk about it before the George-and-Linda show starts … I mean before they show up," said Kim, smiling. "I know you too well. If you don't get it off your chest, you'll continue to worry about it and not enjoy your special night."

"Okay, as long as we can stop talking about it once they show up," said Jack. "George and Linda have been helping me get to the point where I know how to get started saving for retirement and for my dream, but I don't know the first thing about investing."

"Well, let me explain the basics," said Kim.

*　　　　　*　　　　　*

There are a countless number of options of what we can do with our money. We've probably heard or read about many of them.

When we think about investments, however, we first need to understand what it is that we are doing with our money.

- *If we buy stocks*, we are buying a small piece of a company. We become an owner of that company and make money over time when the company grows its profits. As owners, we may also lose money when the company's profits decline over time.

- *If we buy bonds*, we are lending our money to a company or a government and making money on the interest they pay us for giving them a loan. As lenders, we may also lose money if the borrower gets into trouble and is not able to pay us back the money we gave them or the interest they owe us.

- *If we keep our money in a cash investment*, we are typically lending our money for a very short term to a company or a government, and we make money on the interest they pay us for giving them a very short-term loan.

Believe it or not, that's it. Most services provided by financial-service organizations are pretty much products that combine these three basic ingredients. For example, if we buy a mutual fund, we are really just hiring an investment manager to invest our money in stocks, bonds, or cash. If we hire an advisor, we are hiring a professional to choose the investment manager who will invest our money in stocks, bonds, or cash.

*   *   *

"Simple enough," said Jack. "But how am I supposed to know how to build the right kind of portfolio?"

"Jack, that's a soft pitch and you're expecting me to respond with a homerun," said Kim, imitating a baseball player about to swing. "You need to choose investment portfolios that give you the most satisfaction without too much indigestion."

Kim took an imaginary swing and held her hands above her head triumphantly.

"Oh great, more cute ideas," groaned Jack.

"Jack," Kim said, taking a seat across from Jack. "I am quite serious."

$$*\qquad\qquad *\qquad\qquad *$$

Kim is serious, indeed. Those are wise words for a young investment research analyst. When we think about investing our money and can see through the fog and confusion of the endless list of options, we find out that there are really nine options for how to invest our money. Each of the nine circles in the chart below represents the best well-diversified portfolio for different levels of risk that we can have for our investments.[8] The percentage inside the circle represents how much of the portfolio is invested in stocks (with the balance invested in bonds and cash investments).

---

8 A portfolio is defined as a group of investments that are put together to avoid having all the "eggs in one basket." To create well-diversified portfolios, the financial services industry uses multiple techniques, including simulating how the group of investments would have performed, as a group, based on the historical performance of financial markets. It is important to keep in mind that different types of accounts, such as IRAs, brokerage accounts, or 401(k)s are just the "container" and the portfolio is the group of investments inside the container.

When we invest, the most important decision that we need to make is the selection, from these nine options, of the right portfolio for us. The selection criterion is simple. Staying committed to our decision is what makes great investors.

Here is the selection criterion: we need to choose the portfolio that gives us the most satisfaction without giving us more indigestion than we can handle. For maximum satisfaction, we can choose one of the three spicy portfolios; let's just be aware that they come with a higher risk of indigestion—that is why we call them spicy portfolios. Just like choosing a meal, it can be satisfying to have spicy food, but we need to make sure that we can handle the risk of indigestion. Satisfaction really means how we expect our money to grow over time.

The chart above represents the value of $10,000 invested long-term. The $10,000 invested in the spicy portfolios would have grown to more than $1.2 million— much higher than what our money would have grown to if it was invested in the basic or mild portfolios.[9]

---

9   Source: *Ibbotson* and *Zephyr StyleADVISOR* (historical small-cap stocks performance from *Ibbotson* used as primary performance proxy for the small/mid-cap stock investment group). This example is based on the historical performance of financial markets. It uses the 80 percent stock allocation for the spicy

From a satisfaction perspective, we want to be aggressive and invest long-term in a portfolio that has a higher percentage of stock. This is the easy part. The difficult question is whether we can handle the indigestion when stock markets get tough.

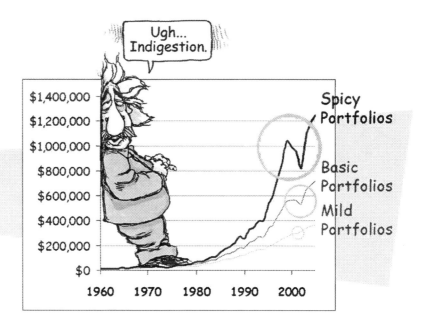

If we had invested in one of the spicy portfolios, we would have seen our account lose close to a quarter of a million dollars during the "dot-com bubble" burst. Could we

_____

portfolios, the 50 percent stock allocation for the basic portfolios, and the 20 percent stock allocation for the mild portfolios. While history provides valuable insights, keep in mind that past performance is no guarantee of future results.

stomach that kind of decline and remain committed to our spicy portfolio? This is the most important question that we need to answer in order to select the right portfolio.

*   *   *

"This is all really a big help. Sorry I reacted the way I did. I thought you were playing with me," said Jack.

"Actually, I'm totally serious," continued Kim. "Most people don't take the time to figure out if they can handle risk and end up investing with their emotions."

*   *   *

Unfortunately, investing for most of us leads to an emotional reaction. When the stock markets are having a bad time and everything is going down, we want to get out and sell our investments. When the stock markets are having a good time and everything is going up, we want to get in and invest more.

Investing by following our emotions leads us to buy at high prices and sell at low prices, which is the opposite of the buy low-sell high discipline that leads to investment success. *Emotions are an investor's worst enemy.*

*   *   *

"Jack, all of this is to clarify one simple concept, so pay attention," explained Kim. "The best investors don't have magic powers. They have an investment recipe that they follow. They establish and commit to one investor style and invest with discipline."

*   *   *

We want to invest with discipline. However, investing with discipline is not a natural behavior to most of us. If we want to invest with discipline, we need to establish an investor style. Our investor style, for example, is our ability to remain committed to our chosen portfolio during times of declining markets. It is our ability to view declining markets as an opportunity to buy, not sell.

During our twenties, we should start by investing our retirement money in the 100-percent spicy portfolio and the money we are saving to build prosperity in the 70-percent spicy portfolio and work hard to establish an investor style.[10]

---

10 This starting point is based on the assumption that an investor in their twenties investing for retirement with discipline and a long-term mindset is better off with a portfolio having the highest possible allocation to stocks. If we are uncomfortable starting with the 100-percent spicy portfolio, the next best option is to start investing for retirement with the 80-percent spicy portfolio. The starting point for the portfolio for the money we are saving to build prosperity is based on the assumption that money saved to build prosperity is typically spent in a combination of short-term (less than seven years) and long-term (seven or more years) needs. If most of the money we are sav-

To begin establishing our investor style, we need to prepare ourselves mentally for the down-markets so we can train ourselves to handle the indigestion.

We need to become aware of the historical behavior of stock markets so we have an appreciation of the normal ups and downs of the market. If we look at the historical year-to-year behavior of the stock market, we'll find out that it's erratic at best, which makes many investors prone to emotional investing. If we look at the historical behavior in increments of ten years (i.e., buy-and-hold for

---

ing to build prosperity is to be spent in short-term needs, one of the basic portfolios may be more appropriate.

ten years), we will find out that the stock market rewards those who invest with discipline.

Over fifty years, as the chart above shows, there hasn't been a single ten-year period when investing (and holding for ten years) in the 100-percent or the 70-percent spicy portfolio would give us indigestion—cause us to lose money.

On the other hand, if we had not prepared for down-markets and invested emotionally year to year—getting in and out of the market—we would have experienced a roller coaster ride with fourteen years of indigestion, or fourteen years of losing money.[11]

We won't know if we have been successful establishing an investor style until we put our investor style through the test—i.e., experience down-markets and have the discipline to remain committed.

If we experience down-markets and remain committed to the 100-percent spicy portfolio for the retirement money and to the 70-percent spicy portfolio for the money we are saving to build prosperity, then we are on our way to establishing our investor style. On the other hand, if we experience down-markets and take our money out of the stock market, we may have more work to do before we can establish our investor style.

First, we need to take a close look at the level of satisfaction that we'll be giving up in the long term by choosing to

---

11 Source: *Ibbotson* and *Zephyr StyleADVISOR* (historical small-cap stocks performance from *Ibbotson* used as primary performance proxy for the small/mid-cap stock investment group). The chart uses the historical performance of the 100-percent spicy portfolio. While history provides valuable insights, keep in mind that past performance is not a guarantee of future results.

move down to the basic portfolios. There is a great cost to move down to the basic portfolios if you are in the early years of your career. In our example of the $10,000 invested long-term, the cost is more than half a million dollars.

However, there is a greater cost in not having an investor style that allows us to invest with discipline because we'll continue to invest with our emotions. If we conclude that we cannot handle the indigestion, then we need to invest our retirement money in the 60-percent basic portfolio and the money we are saving to build prosperity in the 50-percent basic portfolio.

We won't know if we have been successful establishing an investor style until we experience up-markets and have the discipline to avoid moving back to the spicy portfolios. If we are able to remain committed to the basic portfolio while everyone else is celebrating their greater success investing in the spicy portfolios, then we are on our way to establish our investor style. On the other hand, if the temptation is too great and we move back to the spicy portfolios, we have failed to establish an investor style.

*   *   *

"Jack, I know you. I would expect that you'll find your investor style rather quickly," said Kim. "I really think you can be a great investor."

"Probably so," said Jack confidently.

*   *   *

Great investors have an investor style that they have developed and tested over time. They are very aware that a large number of investors invest with their emotions. They recognize that the year-to-year behavior of the market reflects, to a large extent, the effects of emotional investors. They avoid reacting to the ups and downs of the "herd" of emotional investors and stick to their investor style. They believe that a steady pace forward with a tested investor style is the most successful approach to investing.

Learning to gain maximum satisfaction without experiencing too much indigestion is the most important and difficult step in developing our investor style. It is most difficult because we have to learn to ignore the influence of the herd of emotional investors—including an emotional media. Persuasive news stories can range from "the sky is falling" in the event of a down-market, to stories of "the sky is the limit" at times of up-markets.

*   *   *

Just as Kim was about to continue talking to Jack about investments, the doorbell rang. Jack walked toward the door feeling a bit more confident. His financial recipe was taking shape. Now he needed to find out how to select quality investments to include in his spicy portfolios.

Four

Balance

There are big differences between investing, treasure hunting, and crystal-ball betting. Let's become proficient at investing first.

The elevator ride to Jack's apartment on the twentieth floor felt like an eternity for George and Linda. They met by the elevator doors and politely greeted each other after each arriving twenty minutes late in order to dodge each other.

Opening the door, Jack was shocked to see George and Linda standing together. Linda was quick to set the record straight, explaining to Jack that she and George just happened to run into each other outside of the elevator.

Watching the two of them walk in together, Jack was more than a little afraid that having George and Linda in the same room was a gamble and was quietly hoping that his plan to enlist their help in preparing tonight's meal wasn't a recipe for disaster.

"So, Jack," said George, "how's the recipe coming along?"

"Just be patient, and you'll be enjoying it soon."

"I'm talking about money, Jack."

Jack quickly tried to change the subject, explaining his plan for their meal together. "I'm not going to be the one doing the cooking tonight," explained Jack. "I'm going to be giving you guys a cooking lesson."

"So, George," said Linda, ignoring Jack's attempt to redirect the conversation, "I understand that you've been giving Jack pretty naïve advice about his career."

"I have no idea what you're talking about," said George with a playful smile on his face.

"Well, I was hoping that after all these years in the real world, you would finally figure out that career success is more than just following your passions and dreams."

"You know, Linda, you're right," said George. "Of course it is more than just following your passions and dreams. But it's also a lot more than just being an opportunist."

"You, more than anyone else in this room, should know that it's all about opportunity," said Linda, firing back at George. "Isn't that right, Mr. Entrepreneur?"

"That's just a little too simple," said George.

*　　　　*　　　　*

As a review, building wealth is about managing our careers and the money we create with our careers. While we have been focusing primarily on discussing how we need to manage the money we create, it's worthwhile to take a short detour to shed some light on the interesting debate between George and Linda.

Managing our careers is a process that starts by identifying what makes us successful. Do we see some early success in our careers because we commit to what we are passionate about, or do we tend to figure out how to get ourselves into the middle of the right opportunities?

It may take sometime to figure out the answer to this question; however, it is important that we get an answer so we know how to balance the way we manage our career. If we find, like George, that we are successful because we commit to our passions, we need to become disciplined at pursuing the right opportunities. On the other hand, if we find that we are opportunity-focused, like Linda, we need to find a way to develop a passion for the work we do.

The right balance between passion and opportunity is just the first step. Combining that balance with a life-long discipline to continuously build skills that make us unique and the discipline to get things done (i.e., execute plans) is the key to managing our careers.

*   *   *

"Guys!" shouted Jim, forcing himself into the conversation. "You are both wrong and you are both right."

"What?" asked George, surprised to hear Jim enter the conversation.

"Take a look at me," said Jim. "You both know that I became an artist because of my passion …"

"So I guess you're saying that I'm right," said George, eyeing Linda.

"You should let me finish," said Jim, "because I know that passion drives my career. I have to be extra disciplined to make sure that I pursue the right opportunities with my art. When passion drives your career, it's easy to get blinded, to lose touch with reality, and walk right off the cliff. On the other hand, if you drive your career based entirely on opportunity, you are likely to get burnt out."

"Good point," said George.

"Let's get started with this meal," said Jack, seeing a window of opportunity to get George and Linda working together on something where he could keep an eye on them. "George and Linda, you'll be in charge of preparing the tenderloin. Kim and Jim, you guys are in charge of the side dishes."

"Well, Jack, I'm still ready for that recipe we were talking about earlier," said George with a smile.

"You've had all day to figure it out," said Linda.

"Let's not get distracted here," said Jack. "This is a *cooking* lesson."

"Well, you've got to at least tell us what you've come up with," said Linda, who was already reading the recipe and organizing the tenderloin ingredients in front of her and George on the counter.

"Okay," said Jack. "I think I'm almost there. I just need to figure out how to select quality investments to include in my portfolios."

"Just follow the doctor's orders, Jack," said Kim, smiling.

"When did all my friends start acting so cute?" asked Jack, rolling his eyes.

          *   *   *

Now that we have selected the portfolios for our retirement money and for the money we are saving to build prosperity, we need to decide the type of investments we want to include in each portfolio. The approach to selecting the investments is quite straightforward—just follow the doctor's advice: select a well-diversified portfolio, similar to a balanced meal, that includes the five basic investment groups.

What's important is that we know what we are doing with our money when we include each of the five invest-ment groups in our portfolio. In a simpler way, when we invest, we can either lend money or become an owner. With the portion of our portfolio that is invested in cash or bonds, we are lending money. With the portion of our portfolio that is invested in the foreign, small/mid-cap, and large-cap stocks, we are becoming owners.

When we invest in the cash and bonds investment groups, we are, in effect, lending money to someone and getting back a promise that the loan will be paid back with interest.

The investment community uses the term *fixed income* to refer to these investment groups. This term reflects the fact that you are engaging in a prespecified (fixed) agreement within a loan contract.

With the cash investment group, we give a loan to be paid back in less than one year (typically ninety days) to a sound borrower, such as a bank, the U.S. government, or a large profitable corporation. It's pretty safe to assume that the loan will be paid back with interest. For instance, there's not much risk that the government is going to go bankrupt in a year. Worst case, if the government runs into trouble, they can raise taxes to pay us back (which as we know, they do quite well—and often!). This very low-risk investment tends to have a small interest rate that barely covers the rate of inflation because the borrower is offering a safe investment sought by many.

With the bonds-investment group, we give a loan to be paid back in more than one year. The borrower (company or government) has a legal and contractual obligation to pay us back the loan plus interest. Typically, the interest rate paid by bonds is higher because our money is tied up longer and we assume additional risk since conditions may change that would preclude the borrower from paying back the loan.

The investment community uses the term *equity* to refer to the large-cap, small/mid-cap, and foreign stock investment groups.[12] The use of this term refers to the fact that our money is used to buy a very small piece of a company through buying shares of stock. In other words, we become one of the owners of the company. As owners, we make money when the company does well and grows its profits.

Generally, large companies, which we can recognize for having products that are part of our daily lives, tend to be more predictable and stable in their ability to consistently earn a profit. Over the years, they have built a large set of products and services that they sell to a large base of clients. They can grow their profits by launching new products and services or finding new clients. However, the larger the company, the more they need to sell new products and services and find new clients to make their profits grow in a meaningful way—in other words, to make our money grow in a meaningful way.

Small and midsized companies are less predictable and stable in their ability to make money given their smaller base

---

12 *Cap* is a short name for capitalization. Capitalization is the total value of a company and is calculated by multiplying the number of shares outstanding of a company times the market price of each share. The terms *large-cap, medium-cap,* or *small-cap* are the same as the terms large-size company, medium-size company, or small-size company.

of products, services, and clients. However, relatively smaller successes with new products, services, and new clients can make a big difference to their profits, and our money!

What we should expect when investing in foreign companies is no different than what we should expect as an owner of large, midsized, or small United States companies. We expect to see the profitability of foreign companies increase over time. What's different is that we are making a decision to become an owner of a company in a foreign land that is creating products and services mainly for international clients, and this makes the investment more difficult to analyze. In addition, we assume additional risks related to currency exchange and unknown foreign political environments.[13] In our new age of globalization, including the foreign stocks investment group in our portfolio is important to constructing a well-diversified portfolio.

*   *   *

"That's a clever way of explaining things," said Jack. "I thought you were pulling my leg again."

---

13 Funds that invest in foreign stocks may be exposed to additional risks, including currency fluctuations, political instability, foreign taxes and foreign regulation, and the potential for illiquid markets. Historically, small-cap and foreign stocks have been more volatile than stocks of large and more established companies.

"Jack, I deal with many clients," said Kim. "You can't imagine how many of them are not even able to do the basics right. They do stupid things with their money thinking that they can outsmart years of experience. They may as well be throwing their money away."

"That sounds a lot like the stupid things people do to their bodies with every new diet craze," said Jack.

"What do you mean by that?" asked George.

"You'd think that most people would take care of their bodies by eating well-balanced meals that include the five major food groups. How many times have we been told in our lives to just eat well, follow the doctor's advice, and eat a balanced meal? But how many people just want to try the latest fad diet?"

"That's a great way of looking at it," said Kim. "I've seen people put all of their money in a single type of investment just because it's the latest craze, even after they've heard a million times that they are supposed to diversify their portfolios."

"Well, I feel like I'm on the right track," said Jack. "But that doesn't tell me what I'm supposed to do once I know which investment groups I want."

*   *   *

Each of the nine portfolios has a unique combination of the investment groups as shown in the table below. When we

spread out our investments and construct a portfolio following this table, we end up with a well-diversified portfolio.[14]

| | Mild Portfolios | | | Basic Portfolios | | | Spicy Portfolios | | |
	0%	20%	30%	40%	50%	60%	70%	80%	100%
Large-Cap	0%	12%	18%	24%	30%	36%	42%	48%	60%
Small/Mid-Cap	0%	4%	6%	8%	10%	12%	14%	16%	20%
Foreign	0%	4%	6%	8%	10%	12%	14%	16%	20%
Total Stock	0%	20%	30%	40%	50%	60%	70%	80%	100%
Cash Equiv.	20%	16%	14%	12%	10%	8%	6%	4%	0%
Bonds	80%	64%	56%	48%	40%	32%	24%	16%	0%
Total	100%	100%	100%	100%	100%	100%	100%	100%	100%

---

14 Spreading your investments, sometimes called broad market
diversification, means that as a prudent investors you believe
that over the long-term the *relative* stock-market valuation of
the different stock investment groups is broadly correct and
you want to avoid greatly over-or under-weighting a particular
investment group relative to its size in the market (with foreign
stock adjusted to account for currency fluctuations, political
instability, foreign taxes and foreign regulation, and the potential for illiquid markets).

Let's assume that we have successfully completed the first step in establishing our investor style—we have made a commitment to invest our retirement money in the 100-percent spicy portfolio and invest the money we are saving to build prosperity in the 70-percent spicy portfolio. All we need to do is select the percentages that we are going to allocate to each of the investment groups from the table above.

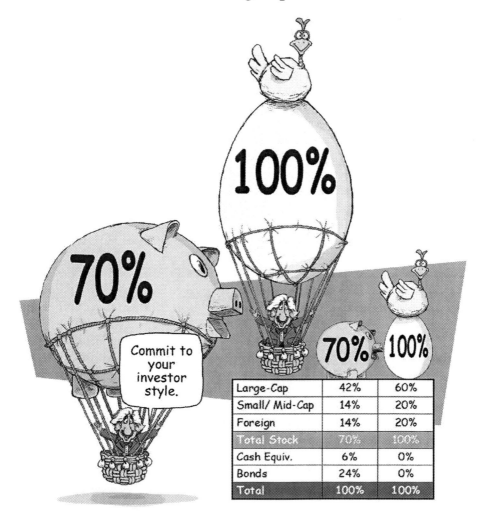

Commit to your investor style.

	70%	100%
Large-Cap	42%	60%
Small/Mid-Cap	14%	20%
Foreign	14%	20%
Total Stock	70%	100%
Cash Equiv.	6%	0%
Bonds	24%	0%
Total	100%	100%

Our next step, then, is to select quality investments for each of the investment groups. In other words, select the companies to lend money to or to buy a piece of.

*   *   *

"Guys, I get all that, but I think we need to be a little more specific," said Jack. "I mean, just because you know how many cups of this or that a recipe calls for, it doesn't mean you can prepare a good meal. You still need to find quality ingredients."

"That's a great point, Jack," said Kim. "Where do you usually go to get quality ingredients?"

"It depends," said Jack. "I go to the farmer's market for some quality ingredients, but for some things I buy name-brand stuff from the supermarket."

"You see, you're already thinking about it the right way."

"I am?" asked Jack, looking completely confused.

*   *   *

During our early years, the most practical approach is probably to use mutual funds.[15] When we use mutual

---

15 The alternatives are to do your own selection of stocks and bonds, which requires a significant commitment to do it right; or, buy other types of financial products such as managed accounts, ETFs or hedge funds, which realistically require the help of a qualified financial advisor.

funds, we are hiring an investment manager to do the selection of stocks and bonds for us.

Investment managers come in two flavors: passive and active investment managers. Investment managers who use the passive approach (often referred to as the indexed approach) lend to organizations or buy a basket of companies without worrying about what is happening inside those organizations. They will usually try to reproduce the contents of an established index, such as the Standard & Poors 500 Stock Index (S&P 500). Investment managers who use the active approach spend a lot of time researching the companies before selecting where to invest. There is a lot of debate about the merits of each approach. Many of those who sell actively-managed mutual funds argue that the active investment approach is superior. Many of those who sell indexed mutual funds argue that their approach is superior.

The real answer is that it depends on the type of investment.

We want to take advantage of the best of both worlds and think in terms of choosing those areas where quality active investment managers have a better chance to do better than the market—i.e., do better than the indexed approach—so we can justify paying more to get better performance. For example, there is a larger number of investment managers looking for the same good investments in the large companies group and using about the same information to find the good investments. In this environment, it's very difficult for active investment managers to find "nuggets" and do better than average on a consistent basis.

On the other hand, active investment managers that specialize in investing in small companies have generally better chances to find "nuggets" others haven't seen since there are fewer of them looking for good investments in these areas, and the information available about these good investments is not as widespread.

As we start to build our portfolios, it makes sense to combine actively-managed mutual funds and indexed mutual funds in our portfolios to take advantage of the best of both worlds. To keep it simple but efficient at the beginning, let's select a couple of actively-managed mutual funds in areas where the investment managers have a better chance to do better than the market, and select the indexed approach for the rest of the investments in the portfolios.[16]

---

16 Categories included in the fifteen-year analysis are: Large-Cap Blend, Intermediate Bond, Small-Cap Blend, Mid-Cap Blend, and Foreign Large Blend. The source of the basic data used for the analysis is *Morningstar*.

As our portfolios grow, we become more experienced with investing, or we get help from a professional advisor, we can look for additional opportunities to use actively-managed mutual funds in other areas of our portfolios where we have a better chance to do better than the indexed approach.

*   *   *

"Jack, think about it this way," said Kim. "Think of indexed funds as ingredients you buy at the farmer's market. Good quality ingredients without the distraction and cost of fancy packaging and advertising."

"That makes sense," said Jack. "Even *I* know that it's not the fancy packaging that makes a quality ingredient. On the other hand, for some ingredients, I know some of the more expensive brands are better."

"Just like some of the actively-managed funds are better, even if they are more expensive," explained Kim.

*   *   *

Now we have the information we need to start building the right portfolios for both our retirement and the money we are saving to build prosperity.

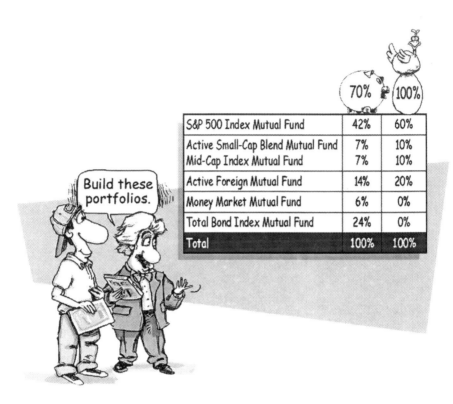

As we will find out later, the way in which we will go about building the portfolios will depend on whether we already have checking and savings accounts, as well as whether our employer offers a 401(k) program.

                    *   *   *

"Kim, obviously you know a lot about investments," said Linda, sliding the stuffed tenderloin into the oven as George held the door open. "I agree with everything that you're saying, but sometimes I think you need to really go after the big investment ideas that can make you rich, or invest in the investment group that you expect will do better in the future."

"I see where you are going," said Kim. "But you need to make a clear distinction between investing, treasure hunting, and crystal-ball betting. I'm sure everyone in this room has read about the guy who invested $5,000 and turned it into $100,000. Of course we all want those investments, who doesn't? However, big bets can come with big losses."

"So what do you usually tell your clients who are looking to do a little treasure hunting or crystal-ball betting?" asked Linda.

"I tell them that if they plan on doing any treasure hunting or crystal-ball betting, they should do it with money that they can afford to lose."

"Actually, I have to admit, I could've used that advice plenty of times in the past," said Linda. "I've spent a lot of my hard-earned money treasure hunting and pursuing crystal-ball bets."

"And did you ever manage to hit the jackpot?" asked Kim.

"If you're asking whether I ever found that pot of gold at the end of the rainbow, no, of course I haven't," said Linda. "It's just so easy to disregard investing the right way and get seduced by the get-rich-quick ideas."

"And you're not alone," said Kim. "But my advice to my clients has always been to become a proficient investor first, and then try their hands at treasure hunting and crystal-ball betting if they have the appetite and the discipline for it. The one bit of advice that usually takes a long time for people to appreciate is to think in terms of becoming rich through *their work and career*, not through their investments."

Jack listened quietly to Kim and Linda and thought about what it would take to become a disciplined investor, how not to be seduced by the promise of richness or fall prey to treasure hunting and crystal-ball betting with his hard-earned money. He imagined that if it could happen to someone as smart as Linda, it could happen to him too. As George and Linda stood near the oven, smiling and talking, Jack couldn't help but wonder if his plan for the evening had actually fallen into place or if this was really just the calm before the storm.

Enlightenment

While we may delegate the day-to-day activities of managing our money, we should never delegate the responsibility of protecting our money.

Jack's recipe for stuffed tenderloin was a success. Jack, George, Kim, Linda, and Jim were seated around the table, enjoying their creation. As the evening unfolded, the five friends brought each other up to date on what they'd been up to since finishing school.

"Talking to you guys is like looking at myself in a mirror," said Linda. "All of you know me so well, better than I even know myself."

"Well, you are kind of predictable," said Jack with a smile.

"Be nice!" said Linda, pretending to throw a napkin across the table at Jack.

"I am. What I mean is that you are a hard-driving person who gets things done. You don't let anyone get in your way. That is just the way you are."

"I'm waiting for the 'but,'" said Linda.

"Okay," said Jack. "Your nature is to be impatient and a bit opportunistic. There's nothing wrong with that as long as you recognize it."

"I'm still waiting for the 'but,'" said Linda with a shrug.

"I bet if we were to ask your co-workers, they would say that you're great at getting yourself involved with the important projects at work."

"Well, I wouldn't call that opportunistic, exactly," said Linda.

"Neither would I," said Jim. "There is nothing wrong with seeking opportunity. Now, if your strength is finding the right opportunities, you need to back it up with the ability to execute. You need to get things done. Otherwise, you'll develop a bad reputation as someone who just jumps from one thing to another always in search of the better opportunity."

"That's right," said Linda. "If you plan to manage your career by being opportunistic and getting involved where value is created in the business, you better get things done. You will be under the microscope every day and everyone will know if you are a difference-maker or simply an opportunist."

"I see what you mean," said Jack.

"And that reminds me of what I've been doing with my money," said Linda. "Which hasn't always worked out for the best. I guess I've been managing my money the same way that I manage my career. I try to be opportunistic."

"I think I know what you mean," said Kim.

"You guys were talking about well-diversified portfolios and investing for the long term," said Linda. "But I assume that financial markets are imperfect enough, so I try to predict what investment groups will do better in the future and move my money to those investments."

"We call that crystal-ball bets or investing with a crystal-ball mentality," said Kim.

*　　　　*　　　　*

Many people will try to persuade us that we are better off investing using a crystal-ball mentality. Let's take a look. Let's pretend that we have a crystal ball. What we have below is a chart that shows how well each basic investment group has done over time.

For instance, in 1981, cash did the best followed by the small/mid-cap stock group, the bonds group, and foreign stock group. The large-cap stock group did the worst in 1981.[17]

Let's pretend that we have a crystal ball. Let's try to find a pattern from the early years that will help us predict the future in the later years consistently. Take a few minutes to study the enlarged version of the chart in the next page.

---

17 Source: *Ibbotson* and *Zephyr StyleADVISOR* (historical small-cap stocks performance from *Ibbotson* used as primary performance proxy for the small/mid-cap stock investment group).

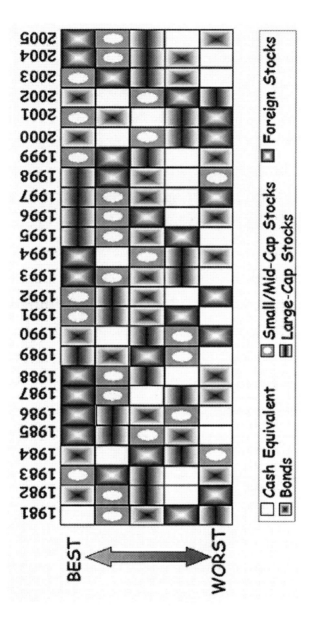

There are *no patterns* to help us predict the future.

We need to use this chart to help us remember to protect our money from the bad habits that many investors follow. Examples: we need to protect our money from the persuasive neighbor who will try to convince us that she has a crystal ball and knows what investments will do better in the future; we need to protect our money from the water-cooler whisper where the herd of investors meet to share their emotions about the market; and we certainly need to protect our money from brokers, advisors, or other professionals who may have a short-term mentality and are telling us that they know how the markets will perform in the future.

Take a close look at the arrows in the chart below. They represent the behavior of the typical investor who has no investing discipline and invests with a crystal-ball mentality.

That undisciplined investor would have yielded, by 1987, to the water-cooler whisper of "how great it was to put her money in foreign stocks." By 1992, after bad performance of foreign stocks over three years, the investor would move out of foreign stocks only to find out that they did well again in 1993 and 1994.

Undisciplined investors who invest with a crystal-ball mentality usually have the worst timing. They get in at the high point (buy high) and get out at the low point (sell low). Let's remember this chart and know that *no one has a crystal ball*. Let's remember that a well-diversified portfolio that gives us maximum satisfaction without giving us too much indigestion is the best way to invest.

*   *   *

"I guess I have been investing with a crystal-ball mentality," said Linda. "No wonder I've lost so much money."

"Linda, you're not alone," said Kim. "You'd be surprised how many very smart people think that they can outsmart and time the market, invest with a crystal-ball mentality, and end up throwing away their money."

"If you focus on becoming proficient at investing first the right way," continued Kim, "then you'll become smart with investments and appreciate the additional risks you are taking, whether you're treasure hunting or crystal-ball betting."

"I've been lucky with my money," said George. "But I wonder if I could do even better if I delegate the day-to-day activities of investing my money to a professional to do it for me."

*   *   *

At this point, we have all the information we need to develop a common-sense plan to get on track saving and investing. Having a good common-sense plan is an important first step to becoming a smart consumer of financial services. Our second and final step is to choose a provider we can trust to implement the plan.

In choosing a provider, we should first decide if we prefer to manage the plan ourselves or if we are more comfortable delegating management of the plan to a professional. If we choose to implement the plan ourselves, we need to commit the time and discipline to doing it right. If we choose to hire a professional, we need to make sure that we are delegating the day-to-day management of our money, but not our responsibility to protect our money.

Also, let's keep in mind that professionals tend to like clients who already have accumulated balances in their accounts. If we are just getting started, we may find it easier to just follow the recipes in this book, find a provider offering self-guided services where we can manage the plan ourselves, and later switch to a provider offering managed services, if that is our preference.

There are primarily three reasons to hire a professional: 1) we are not able to shift to a wealth mindset and we need someone to bring discipline into our spending habits; 2) we are not able to establish an investor style and we need the help of a professional to help us establish one; and 3) we want to delegate the day-to-day activity of managing our money.

We should never delegate responsibility over our investments to a professional because we think that a professional has a "better map" to go treasure hunting or a superior crystal ball to go gamble with our money. When we hire a professional, we should expect the professional to follow the sound recipes in this book.

While there will be some differences in the details of their recipes, the overall methodology and investment principles should be consistent.

Delegating to a professional does not mean we can then forget about protecting our money. On the contrary, we need to remain involved and monitor the work of the professional to verify that he or she is continuing to follow the recipes in this book.

Finally, if we experience tough years of declining markets, we should not make the mistake of jumping around hoping for a professional with better recipes. We need to remain committed to a professional who follows the right recipes. The only time we want to change them is when we believe that he or she has stopped following the sound recipes in this book.

*   *   *

"My company is in the business," said Kim. "You can hire us as the professional to manage your plan."

"Why do people typically use your company," asked Jack.

"I think we have built a reputation for being more conservative and taking a long-term perspective of managing the plan," responded Kim. "Different firms add value in different ways. You just need to know what you are getting for what you are paying."

*   *   *

When we delegate the day-to-day activities of managing our money to an advisor, we should be aware that the advisor may emphasize certain investment groups within the philosophy of well-diversified portfolios, or may make small adjustments to the portfolio during an economic cycle.

For instance, the advisor may have a philosophy that emphasizes small and midsize companies. She may argue that over the long term, smaller companies have performed better than larger companies.

A different advisor may emphasize foreign companies because he believes that globalization and the Internet are allowing the rest of the world to close the economic gap with the United States

Those advisors may, for instance, recommend portfolio allocation that differs slightly, at the investment group level, from the nine well-diversified portfolios in this book. As long as the advisor is committed to a philosophy of well-diversified portfolios and the recommendation for each investment group for the spicy portfolios is within (plus or minus) 10 percent of the well-diversified portfolios in this book, those recommendations are okay.

If the recommendation difference for any of the investment groups is larger than (plus or minus) 10 percent, we should be aware that, in essence, the provider is making a bet that a certain investment group will do better in the future. If we want to make a bet on a certain investment group, we need to be certain that we are doing so because we agree with the provider's investment philosophy over the long term and understand the additional risk of indigestion we may be undertaking. More importantly, we need to be certain that we are not just trying to invest with a short-term crystal-ball mentality.

One more thought to keep in mind ...

The trusted advisor may have an investment methodology to enhance our portfolios by replacing some of the indexed mutual funds with actively-managed mutual funds. Advisors who recognize the importance to balance the use of actively-managed mutual funds and index funds where it makes sense should be able to enhance our portfolios. However, it requires a disciplined investment process to find the right active investment managers. The trusted advisor must have a disciplined investment process that provides good insights about the reasons for the actively-managed funds' good performance in the past, more importantly, provides a well-thought-out rationale to justify why she expects that the actively-managed funds will continue to do well in the future once our money is invested in those funds.

*   *   *

"Now that's interesting," said Jim. "I've had some bad experiences with advisors and I'm not quite sure what to think. What do you think, Kim?"

"Well, if you're among two-thirds of the population of investors, you'll seek the help of a financial advisor to manage your money at some point in your life. There's a lot of good help out there from financial advisors, but there's also bad help," answered Kim, looking at Jack and shaking her head in surprise as she watched Linda and George get up from the table and walk out of sight.

*   *   *

If we want to delegate help to a professional, we need to use a trusted advisor. To find the right trusted advisor, it is important that we become familiar with how various advisors try to appeal to potential clients. The three most seductive advisors are the *free advisor, proprietary investments advisor*, and *crystal ball advisor*. Once we are able to spot and avoid the seduction traps set up by each of these advisors, we'll be able to find the right trusted advisor.

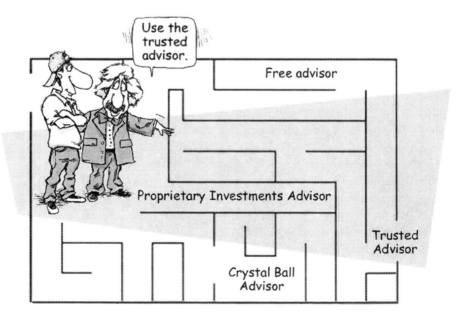

Let's look inside the labyrinth of advisors. Let's imagine ourselves sitting across the table from the free advisor. The free advisor will tell us that his services are absolutely free of charge. Sounds too good to be true? We'd have a right to be suspicious at this point. How could someone provide a service for which other advisors are charging fees? Shouldn't they be destroying the competition? The truth is that the free advisor is receiving compensation for his services—just not from us.

While every advisor should be fairly compensated for their services, it is important that the advisor earns our trust by disclosing the commissions collected from the investments they sell and any potential conflicts. Many advisors acting as selling agents for investment providers get paid a commission for including the provider's investment products in our portfolio and portray their services as "free services." We may find that there is a risk of ending up with expensive low-quality investments in our portfolio because of the advisor's conflict of interest. We just need to remember that there is no such thing as *free investing*.

On the other hand, we might find ourselves discussing our needs with the proprietary investments advisor. The proprietary investments advisor will tell us that he or his firm is an expert, successful with all investment groups and types. A service provider claiming to have the best investments across all investment groups is about as unrealistic as building a sports organization that has a chance to win the Super Bowl, the World Series, the Stanley Cup, and the NBA Championship.

If the advisor wanting to help us requires that we must use only their proprietary investments in our portfolio, we should avoid that advisor.

Lastly—and perhaps the most dubious of all—we may find ourselves talking to the crystal ball advisor. This is probably the most seductive advisor of all. Their stories are exciting and can be very tempting. We need to remember, however, that no one can predict the future. There are no patterns from the past to predict the future on a consistent basis.

We need to make sure we are hiring an advisor who believes that a well-diversified portfolio—not trying to predict the future with a crystal ball—is the best investment philosophy.

*   *   *

"Whoa! What is that all about?" muttered George after being pinned against the wall in the hallway by a kiss from Linda.

"That's opportunity," Linda barely responded before being kissed back.

"And what is that?" asked Linda, smiling after a long and romantic kiss with George.

"That's passion," smiled back George before putting his arms around Linda and kissing her like the old college days.

"It's funny to see how our personalities shape the ways we manage our money," said Jack, leaning back in his chair as he watched Linda and George walk back into the room holding hands.

"You're so right," said Linda, looking at Jack with a big smile. "You have to be so aware and honest about who you are and what gives you satisfaction ... I mean, what makes you successful. There is nothing wrong with using it to your advantage. That is the easy part."

"The hard part is to recognize that there is always a better way," said George, smiling at Linda.

"The hard part is to recognize that balance is the better way," said Jim, still trying to process the sudden change of events.

"And staying committed to it," added Kim, happy to see George and Linda together again.

"I'm so glad that we got together," said Jack. "It's good to be with such great friends. And George ... now I see. It is all a *recipe*!"

Six

Jack's Recipe Notes

Develop a plan you can afford, and commit to that plan.

With complete confidence in his skills as a sous-chef and in financial matters, Jack began his lifelong dream of building a chain of gourmet restaurants the very next day—a lifelong journey of enjoying both personal and financial wealth. Jack became a very successful sous-chef and was quickly promoted to head chef. He developed a reputation for preparing the finest stuffed tenderloin in town.

Among his co-workers and friends at the restaurant, for whom Jack took every opportunity to help in developing their own recipes for financial success, Jack earned the nickname "Financial Chef."

Below are the notes that Jack created to help his young friends and fellow employees at the restaurant to get on track saving and investing. His notes are organized so that you can find them helpful regardless of what line of work you are in, and exactly where you are in your career.

You can use Jack's notes to create your own recipe. As you create your plan, keep in mind that the best plan is a plan that you can afford and to which you can commit.

While this book provides straightforward details for an affordable plan, what you can afford and commit to will vary from reader to reader. However, you may be surprised to see just what you can afford once you make the commitment to build wealth.

Read Jack's notes and select the one that fits your situation to get started:

Note#1: **I'm just getting started and my employer doesn't offer a 401(k)-type plan to save for retirement.**

Check List:

- ☐ **Step 1:** Open an interest-bearing savings account and a checking account with a reputable local bank if you currently do not have them. Compare the services offered by at least three banks to make sure you get a good interest rate in the savings account.

- ☐ **Step 2:** Ask your employer to split your paycheck and automatically deposit, ideally, 15 percent of your pre-tax salary into the savings account for your retirement and prosperity savings. Have the remaining balance deposited into the checking account for your living expenses.

- ☐ **Step 3:** Accumulate at least $3,000 in the savings account before looking for an investment provider to start building your portfolios. While investment providers may require a lower minimum to open the account, for quality mutual funds that you will want to add to your portfolio, $3,000 is about the typical minimum investment.

☐ **Step 4:** Once you have accumulated at least $3,000, sign up for a Roth IRA retirement account with a quality investment provider.

Steps 5, 6, and 7 (if you prefer to keep it as simple as possible, even if it's not the optimal solution):

☐ **Step 5:** Tell the provider that you are looking for an *asset allocation mutual fund* (also called *lifestyle* or *lifecycle* fund[18]) that provides an allocation that matches—as closely as possible—the 100-percent spicy portfolio. Just tell them that you are looking for an allocation that includes 60 percent large-cap stocks, 20 percent small/mid-cap stocks, and 20 percent foreign stocks. If they don't have it, do not settle for any allocation that provides less satisfaction than the 80-percent spicy portfolio.

☐ **Step 6:** Continue to accumulate an additional $3,000 in your savings account to get ready to open your investment account for the money you plan to invest

---

18 Lifecycle funds have the unique characteristic of adjusting the allocation to more conservative allocation over time (i.e., become less satisfying portfolios with a lower risk of indigestions).

to build prosperity. Once you accumulate your second $3,000, sign up for a general investing account.

☐ **Step 7:** This time, tell the provider that you are looking for an asset allocation mutual fund that provides an allocation as close as possible to the 70-percent spicy portfolio. Just tell them that you are looking for an allocation that includes 42 percent large-cap stock, 14 percent small/mid-cap stocks, 14 percent foreign stock, 24 percent bonds, and 6 percent cash equivalent. If they don't have it, don't settle for an allocation that provides less satisfaction than the 60-percent basic portfolio.

And that's it! Once you have opened the accounts and purchased the initial investment, the minimums for additional investments are much lower and in the range of $1,000 or less. Just repeat the process to continue growing your retirement and prosperity investment account.

Keep in mind that you are trading speed and simplicity for a good but not optimal portfolio, which is okay to get started. You'll have plenty of time to update your portfolio as your accounts grow.

If you have chosen to invest with a provider such as Vanguard (www.vanguard.com), a company that built its reputation as a provider of index funds, the asset allocation mutual fund is likely to have index funds for the small-cap and foreign stock investments, which is okay if you want to start with a simple approach.

On the other hand, if you have chosen to invest with a provider such as Fidelity (www.Fidelity.com) or T. Rowe Price (www.troweprice.com), companies that built their reputations as providers of actively-managed mutual funds, the asset allocation mutual fund is likely to have actively-managed mutual funds for the large-cap, mid-cap, and bonds investments, which also works for this simple approach to get started.

Finally, by choosing an asset allocation mutual fund, you may be relying on the proprietary investments of a single provider to manage all the investment groups, which, again, is okay if you want to keep it simple early on.

*   *   *

Steps 5, 6, and 7 (if you would rather go through the necessary steps to get the optimal solution as soon as possible):

☐ **Step 5:** Tell the provider that you want to invest in their least expensive S&P 500 Index mutual fund. Ask the provider for a no-load fund that has an expense ratio less than 0.4 percent and ideally closer to 0.2 percent.

☐ **Step 6:** Now focus on accumulating the next $3,000 in your savings account so you can get ready to open your prosperity investment account. Once you've accumulated $3,000, sign up for a general investing account and invest the money in the S&P 500 Index mutual fund.

☐ **Step 7:** Continue to accumulate an additional $3,000 in your savings account. Go ahead and invest the additional $3,000 in the retirement account again so you get diversification as soon as possible. This time, ask the provider to give you their least expensive mid-cap index mutual fund. Ask the provider for a no-load fund that has an expense ratio of less than 0.5 percent and ideally closer to 0.25 percent.

While this is a slower process to build your portfolios, you are focusing on building the optimal portfolio from the very beginning. The process continues with each investment until there is enough money in the accounts to match the allocations suggested in the book for the 100-percent spicy portfolio for the retirement money and the 70-percent spicy portfolio for the money you are saving to build prosperity.

Keep in mind that the expense ratio of the total index bond mutual fund should be less than 0.5 percent and ideally closer to 0.25 percent. Also, keep in mind that for the active small-cap blend mutual fund and the active foreign mutual fund, the expense ratios should be less than

1.5 percent and 1.7 percent respectively. When selecting the active funds, request funds that have *consistently* performed above average for the last three and five years and have not changed the investment manager during this period.

If you have already accumulated balances in existing accounts, determine if your current provider allows you to build the portfolio as specified above. If not, you may consider other providers that have built a reputation as supermarkets of mutual funds, such as Schwab (www. schwab.com) or TDAmeritrade (www.tdameritrade.com). Since you have already accumulated balances, you should be able to build your portfolios more quickly.

*   *   *

Note #2: **My employer offers a 401(k) type account.**

Check List:

- □ **Step 1:** Sign up for your company's 401(k) plan with your very first paycheck and elect to have, ideally, 10 percent of your pre-tax salary invested in the Roth 401(k) option of your plan.

- □ **Step 2:** In your 401(k) enrollment form, select the right investments to build a 100-percent spicy portfolio (60 percent to the S&P 500 Index mutual fund, 10 percent to an active small-cap blend mutual fund,

10 percent to the mid-cap index mutual fund, and 20 percent to an active foreign mutual fund).

☐ **Step 3:** Open an interest-bearing savings account and a checking account with a reputable local bank if you currently do not have them. Compare the services offered by at least three banks to make sure you get a good interest rate in the savings account.

☐ **Step 4:** Ask your employer to split your paycheck and automatically deposit 5 percent of your pre-tax salary in the savings account for the money you are saving to build prosperity with the balance deposited in the checking account for your living expenses.

☐ **Step 5:** Accumulate at least $3,000 in the savings account before looking for an investment provider to start building your portfolios for the money you are saving to build prosperity.

☐ **Step 6:** Once your $3,000 is ready, sign up for a general investing account and invest the money in the S&P 500 Index mutual fund.

☐ **Step 7:** As you accumulate the minimum investment levels in your savings account, continue to invest in the additional investment groups to build your portfolio for the money you are saving to build prosperity.

There are a couple of situations that you may encounter with your employer's 401(k)-type plan. First, they may not yet offer a Roth 401(k) plan option. If that is the case, you may need to start with the regular 401(k) plan option and check with the employer about their plan to add the Roth 401(k) option. As soon as that option is added, you can start investing in the Roth 401(k) option. Second, the 401(k)-type plan may not offer all the investments that you need to build the right portfolio as described in this book. For instance, they may not offer the S&P 500 Index mutual fund. Instead, they may offer an actively-managed large-cap fund. Just beware of coming up short in the lineup of investments in the plan. At this point you have no option but to use the investment options offered by the employer. You can, however, let them know that they should add the missing investment options to the plan so you are able to build your preferred portfolio.

About the Author

Christian Echavarria is the founder and CEO of ALTO Group, a business development and investment company. He is also a cofounder of Invesmart, a financial services company advising and investing over $6 billion in corporate and individual assets.

Additionally, as a consultant with McKinsey & Company, Echavarria advised senior executives at Fortune 500 companies on strategy and corporate development. Echavarria holds an MBA from the Wharton School of the University of Pennsylvania.

Echavarria enjoys mountain biking in his hometown of Sewickley, Pennsylvania, where he lives with his wife, Laurel, daughters Lauren and Andrea, and son, Alex.

978-0-595-67904-1
0-595-67904-8

Printed in the United Kingdom
by Lightning Source UK Ltd.
130785UK00002B/31/A